THE PERSON OF CHRIST

Contents

His Deity 7

The Manhood of Christ 12

His Incarnation 15

His Sinless Life 18

His Death 22

His Resurrection 26

His Ascension 30

His Enthronement 34

His Present Ministry 38

His Second Coming 42

His Second Advent and Millennial Reign 45

His Deity

This series of articles will be of a devotional nature and will focus on the fundamental truths regarding our blessed Lord Jesus Christ. It is most refreshing and confirmatory for Christians to go over these great themes in the light of the teaching of Scripture, and every Christian should do this at some time. It is all the more greatly needed in the days in which we live, when the person of Christ is being assailed by modernists as well as the Cults. Even those in so called evangelical circles today are either denying certain doctrines of Christ or casting doubts on them. Christ is the touchstone of all doctrine. We should always ask when hearing teaching of which we are unsure "How does this affect the truth of the Person of Christ?". "Does it undermine His person and work at Calvary in any way?". Christ is the yardstick by which we should measure all teaching. The apostles built their teaching up on the solid foundation of the wholesome words of the Lord Jesus Christ (1 Tim 6:3). What He taught provided a standard for apostolic teaching. It is only by continual occupation with Christ's teaching and that of the apostles that believers will be preserved in a healthy way spiritually. He is the acid test of all teaching. Paul, for example, in combating fundamental error being taught to the Colossian believers sums up the heresy threatening them by saying it is "not after Christ" (Col 2:8). In what lovely fashion he dismisses error! He does not there discuss the system in great detail, but sets over against it the rule of Christian faith. This is a good guide for us. The first truth it is important to consider is the deity of Christ. Is the Christ of the Bible God? Can we be confident that Christ is more than a man? Is the Christian justified in believing Christ to be equal with God? Is He a fragment of the divine, or is He the fullness of deity? These questions must be answered, for they are crucial to our Christian faith, but they must be answered from the Holy Scriptures. There are many passages in the NT which we could look at on this precious subject, but we will concentrate on Hebrews chapter 1, in which great chapter there is clearly set forth most convincing proofs of the deity of Christ; proofs that are in harmony with, and supported by, other parts of the word of God.

Using Hebrews 1 then as a basis, let us notice the many aspects in which the deity of our Saviour is accepted, presupposed and upheld. The truths concerning the deity of Christ are in each case brought before us in a threefold way.

1. DIVINE NAMES ARE ASCRIBED TO HIM

In v.5 Christ is addressed as "my Son"; in v.8 as "God"; in v.10 as "Jehovah". In v.5 God is cited from Psalm 2:7 as addressing His Son, "Thou art my Son". Notice that this is in a section of the chapter where Christ is contrasted with angels, They are but servants (ministers), while He is the Son. The singular title "Son" is never used of angels or men in the OT. Angels are sometimes called "sons of God" (Psalm 29:1 & 89:6), but to no one but Christ is the title given individually in all the long time of revelation. This relation of Christ to God is peculiar and not shared by others. The Sonship of Christ in the NT Scriptures implies His co-equality to God. For example, John the apostle in his writings never calls believers "sons", but "children". He reserves this title for Christ alone. The Jews knew that when our Lord spoke of Himself as the Son of God it was an unqualified claim to deity. Hence they took up stones to stone Him (John 10:24-31). The testimony of Hebrews 1 to the deity of Christ is overwhelming. In vv. 1-4 it is of what God says OF His Son, but in vv. 5-14 it is what God says TO His Son. In v. 8 we have the very language of God addressing the Lord Jesus- "Thy throne, O God, is for ever and ever". This quotation is from Psalm 45, a messianic Psalm. How convincing this should be. God Himself calls His Son "God". Let us not forget that, in the context here, the writer is showing the fitness of the Lord Jesus to be the final revealer of God to men. Only one possessed of full deity is perfectly qualified to reveal God. In v.10 Christ is seen as Jehovah from Psalm 102:25-27. If any one should doubt that the Jesus of the NT is the Jehovah of the OT then a look at the Hebrew writer's use and application of this Psalm to Christ should be enough to settle the matter. The immediate context of the Psalm makes his use of it all the more remarkable in that vv. 23-24 picture Christ in His path to the cross, "He weakened my strength in the way, He shortened my days...". Here we have the Lord Jesus in His path of humiliation as true man and yet the next two verses of the Psalm clearly set forth His omnipotent deity in creation. Thus the weakened Sufferer is the sovereign Creator. There is only one person in God's universe in whom both seemingly incredible and irreconcilable aspects could be seen, and that is the Lord Jesus Christ.

2. DIVINE WORKS ARE ATTRIBUTED TO HIM

In v.2 Christ is said to have made the worlds (or aions). In v.3 He upholds all things. Then in v.10 He has laid the foundation of the earth. Here we have Christ's threefold work in creation. He is the Creator of the world. He has indeed formed the ages. Presently in His providential activity He upholds all things in creation. In the beginning it was Christ who laid the earth's foundation. These works could not be attributed to a creature, however great such a person was. Pondering these statements there is only one inevitable conclusion; Christ is distinct from creation. He existed prior to creation. He is indispensable to creation. He is therefore God. A creature who is also a creator is an impossible conclusion! The creatorial glory of Christ reaches backward to before creation and reaches forward to the time when all creation will be His as the Heir (v.2). This great chapter teaches that Christ is more than man.

3. DIVINE ATTRIBUTES ARE APPLIED TO HIM

Our glorious Lord possesses all the attributes of deity. Every attribute seen in Jehovah is found in Christ. Do notice three divine attributes relative to Christ. In v.8 He is eternal; "Thy throne, O God, is for ever and ever". Our Lord had no beginning. He was free from the succession of time. In fact He is the cause of time. He is the eternally pre-existent One. This pre-existence certainly does not mean that He just existed in the mind of God before He came into the world. No! Colossians 1:17 declares "He is before all things". The pre-existent Christ is personal, *"He"*; absolute, *"is"*; eternal, *"before"*; supreme, *"all things"*. So the Lord Jesus in the incarnation continued to be what He ever had been from all eternity; God. In v.10 Christ is omnipotent; "the heavens are the work of thine hands". Here the Lord Jesus is clearly brought before us as the Creator of the world. He did not become a creature, because He became a man in His own creation. The Lord Jesus was not a created being. Eight times in the NT the Lord Jesus is referred to as the Creator. To Him belong might and power and these were put forth in bringing the world into being. Then in vv.11-12 it is wonderful to see that the Lord Jesus Christ is unchangeable; "Thou remainest"; "Thou art the same". At the end of the OT God has said "I am the Lord (Jehovah), I change not" (Mal 3:6). What God is, Christ is. It has been well said "A Saviour who is not quite God is like a bridge broken at the further end".

4. DIVINE PREROGATIVES ARE ACCORDED HIM

In v.6 the Lord Jesus is seen as the object of worship; "let all the angels of God worship Him". In a future day when Christ will reign in His millennial kingdom the angels will worship Him. This acceptance of worship by Christ in itself shows His deity. When the Lord was here on earth on more than one occasion He was worshipped. In John 20 when He stood in the upper room, having risen from the dead, He was worshipped by Thomas and called "God". Notice here that He is called "God" in the presence of ten witnesses and that He accepted the worship and language of Thomas. The Lord Jesus said not one word to reprove His disciple. The prerogative to receive worship belongs to God, and Christ is equal with God.

Let us go to v.8 to see yet another great aspect concerning the person of Christ. There we delight to observe a further gem of vital truth. Kingship, or rule, belongs to our Saviour. We read of God speaking of the fact that Christ has a throne. Also the "sceptre", the symbol of rule, is spoken of. The Lord has a kingdom. Seven times in the Psalm cited (Psalm 45) the Messiah, our Lord Jesus Christ, is expressly referred to as the King. Now rule is the grand prerogative of God. Many times in the Psalms God is referred to as the King. Take, for example, Psalm 95:3, "for the Lord is a great God, and a great King above all gods". When the Lord Jesus comes back to reign, as He surely will, it is said of Him, "and the Lord shall be king over all the earth" (Zech 14:9). Who is this king? The answer is in v.5 where he says, "the Lord my God shall come…". There is no doubt as to the deity of the King's person in Zechariah's mind and it is hoped that there is no doubt in our minds either.

Finally, in v.3 there is the great statement concerning Christ. It is the seventh important statement as to the person of the Lord in vv.1-3. Here in all its momentous significance, "when he had by himself purged our sins…". Christ, by virtue of His death at Calvary, is said to purge the sins of every believer. Now the forgiveness of sins is the prerogative of God alone. This even the scribes recognised when they said in their unspoken thoughts, "Who can forgive sins but God only?" (Mark 2:7). The Lord had said to the sick of the palsy, "Son, thy sins be forgiven thee", but these scribes who were present in the house were accusing the Lord of blasphemous presumption. Yes, they were right that God only can forgive sin, but they were wrong in thinking that the Lord Jesus was only man. By bringing into the light of open day their unspoken thoughts, and by healing the man, the Lord proved that He was God. Christ had power in the physical realm, but He had power in the spiritual realm, too, in forgiving sin. He has still. The twofold attribute of God in forgiving sin and healing diseases (Ps 103:3) was powerfully expressed and displayed by Christ in the crowded house that day.

Thus, in the doctrine of Hebrews there should be no mistaking the divine prerogatives fully possessed by Christ. Worship, rule and the purging of sin are the rights alone of absolute deity. No one carefully reading all the statements and Scriptures in Hebrews 1 concerning Christ should entertain any doubts as to the fact that Christ is God. If this is true, and it is, then it should have a very profound effect upon our lives. If Christ be God, He deserves our all. CT Studd, one time great cricketer become missionary, said, "If Jesus Christ be God and died for me, then no sacrifice should be too great for me to make for Him".

The Manhood of Christ

In the days of the Apostle John there were already those who were denying the true manhood of the Lord Jesus. So to combat this heresy he writes in his 1st Epistle of the fact that "Jesus Christ is come in flesh" (1 John 4:2&3). He clearly states that those who confess this are of God and those who confess it not are not of God; they are deceivers and manifest the spirit of the antichrist. Such inspired language solemnly reveals the seriousness of wrong teaching concerning the person of Christ. The Saviour in whom the believer trusts is truly man. He did not merely assume manhood in coming into this world of ours. He did not act out the part of a man on the stage of time. He did not just have the appearance of a man. His manhood was PHYSICALLY like that of all men (Rom 8:3), but MORALLY His manhood was unlike that of any other (Heb 4:15). It must never be thought that Christ is two persons in one. Scripture never divides up the Lord Jesus in this way. The manhood that the Lord took in incarnation did not add to Him a fresh personality. The Lord becoming man ever remained the Divine Person that He ever was. It is true to say that the Lord Jesus in the days of His flesh was one Person possessed of both essential deity and true manhood. To illustrate this important point the Lord Jesus said, "Before Abraham was, I am" (John 8:58). He also said, "I will put my trust in Him" (Heb 2:13). These were not two "I"s. The first saying is understood in the light of the Lord's deity. The second in the light of the Lord's manhood. The Person who spoke these words was one – the Son of God. When therefore the Lord became flesh there was no change in His Person. His form was changed– yes. The conditions into which He came were changed–yes, but His Person was ever the same.

THE PROOF OF THE LORD'S MANHOOD
Our Lord had feelings and emotions as a real man and passed through experiences that belong properly to man. In the wilderness when tempted of the devil He was hungry (Matt 4:2). Now hunger is not a consequence of the fall. Had Adam not sinned he would still have been hungry in the Garden of Eden. Hence the food provided by God in the Garden. The Lord Jesus was so

much a man that He was capable of being tired. Look at Him sitting on the well as He meets the woman of Samaria. John tells us He was "wearied with His journey" (John 4:6). What a proof this is of His real manhood. Contrast this with Isaiah's statement of the greatness and omnipotence of God, "The Creator of the ends of the earth, fainteth not, neither is weary" (Isa 40:28). How amazing this is! Does it not show that the Lord willingly accepted the conditions into which He came as a true man? In His eternal deity He never knew weariness, but in His dependent manhood He knew what it was to be tired after a long walk. At the grave of Lazarus He wept (John 11:35). Matthew Henry could write: "Jesus Christ was really and truly man, and partook with the children, not only of flesh and blood, but of a human soul, susceptible of the impressions of joy, and grief, and other affections. Christ gave this proof of his humanity, in both senses of the word; that, as a man, he could weep, and, as a merciful man, he would weep, before he gave this proof of his divinity".

Then the Lord was thirsty both at the well of Sychar and on the cross of Calvary. Again it is amazing to think of One who "measured the waters in the hollow of His hand" (Isa 40:12) asking the woman at the well for a drink. Water is a common basic need of man. Thirst can be an intense human experience. The Lord in His Holy Manhood subjected Himself to such a condition. His manhood was complete in every way. Sleep is a merciful provision of the Creator for man to renew physical and mental powers. And yet the Lord Himself knew what it was to sleep. We see Him in the hinder part of the boat asleep (Mark 4:38). Here is yet another proof of the Lord's real manhood. Another evidence of the Lord's manhood is that He was often found in prayer. Luke in his delightful Gospel shows us the Lord as the dependent Man continually withdrawing into the presence of God in prayer.

The Lord Jesus possessed a real body of flesh that was also capable of pain and suffering. This He felt in all its awfulness. It must not be forgotten that Peter tells us He was put to death "in the flesh" (1 Pet 3:18). The Lord then was not impassive or lacking in emotions and feelings. These seven signs of the Lord's Manhood briefly referred to should be more than enough to prove that He was a real Man with a body, soul and spirit. This should touch the heart and cause the believer to hold firmly to the clear teaching of Scripture.

THE PERFECTION OF THE LORD'S MANHOOD

What we have looked at so far are things that the Lord Jesus was capable of as Man, and yet His Manhood was such that there were things He was incapable of. He was altogether distinct from other men. In the Lord Jesus is found sinless Manhood. Because He was perfect Man He was thoroughly incapable of sin. To say that the Lord could have sinned, though He never did is really to deny His perfect Manhood. Our Lord Jesus came into this world clean and untainted by the effects of the fall of Adam. Matthew writes of the Angel who told Joseph that the Lord was conceived by the Holy Spirit (Matt 1:20). If men try to teach otherwise then they deny the purity of Mary as a virgin and also the truthfulness of the Gospel records. The Lord was free from hereditary depravity and from actual sin. The Lord not only expressly called Himself "Man" (John 8:40), but was personally aware of His own sinlessness. He could say, "which of you convinceth Me of sin?" (John 8:46).

There are many ways in which the Lord's sinless manhood is seen. Think well on the following facts. He never offered a sacrifice for His sins. He never prayed for forgiveness. He never prayed with others. He never prayed for Himself. All men, but He, needed new birth. He could say in His teaching "if YE then, being evil..." (Matt 7:11). How greatly significant that He did not say "WE"! He was the only man who broke the connection between sin and death – the wages of sin is death (Rom 6:23). The Lord in His holy manhood was distinct and different from fallen man.

THE PERMANENCY OF HIS MANHOOD

It is truly wonderful to know that our blessed Saviour in resurrection and exaltation to heaven continues to be man. He did not leave His body in the grave. No, thank God He will remain a man forever. Paul speaking of the Lord's present ministry as Mediator describes Him as the "man Christ Jesus" (1 Tim 2:5). The Lord in resurrection showed He was still a real man. Luke in His Gospel (ch. 24) tells of the Lord walking between seven and eight miles with two disciples and of his eating fish and a honeycomb. The Lord in heaven has a real body. Paul calls it "the body of His glory" (Phil 3:21, Newberry margin). It is right and good to refer to the Lord as the man in the glory. It is true to say that at present the Lord is the only man in heaven with a body. He took His body in incarnation and thereby took manhood to Himself, but in rising from the dead He has taken manhood in His person to the very throne of God. "Could we with anointed eye pierce the unseen, passing the angelic hosts and all the hierarchies of heaven, we should see on the highest pinnacle of the Universe, the throne of the Father, seated at the right hand of the majesty on high, the Son of Man, glorified with the same 'glory which He had with the Father before the world was', no less truly and completely man than in this scene, for 'Jesus Christ is the same yesterday, today and forever'" (W Hoste. Studies In Bible Doctrine, page 47).

His Incarnation

The word "incarnation" is not a scriptural one, but is used by Christians to refer to the wonderful event of the Lord Jesus Christ becoming man. It actually comes from the Latin, in and caro (flesh). It is the act of assuming or becoming flesh. Doctrinally, it refers to the Lord Jesus coming into this world and uniting, in one Person, Godhead and Manhood. This is an amazing truth that is absolutely without parallel in history. It is the great marvel of the Godhead and of eternity. It cannot be explained by natural reasoning, but must be accepted by faith.

Man has been brought into this world in different ways.
1. By creation as in the case of the first man Adam.
2. By formation as is seen in Eve.
3. By generation as is true of all human births.

The outstanding exception to this is our Lord Jesus who was brought into this world by incarnation. In contrast to Adam, the God who brought a motherless woman from the body of a man also brought a fatherless man from the body of a woman – our blessed Lord! This is an overwhelming mystery to our souls, but we believe it and worship our God for it. What really was the incarnation, especially for Christ Himself?

The incarnation of Christ was a stoop. The Lord of glory stepped into time and in so doing became what He had never been before – a dependent yet perfect man. For the Lord this was a real descent. It must not be forgotten that He was the Son of the Highest. His native sphere was Heaven, yet in marvellous condescending grace He who was spirit became flesh, He who was invisible became visible and He who was God became man.

The Lord of glory was born into this world so low down that no babe could ever have been born lower. It is touching to read in Luke that the Lord was wrapped in swaddling clothes (Luke 2:7). Think of the Lord of glory a baby in the arms of Mary and confined to these wrappings. While it is said of both Christ and Adam that they were "made a little lower than the angels" (see Heb 2:7 & 9), yet there is a difference. In Adam's case it did not mean a descent, for he knew no previous existence in Heaven like the

Lord. For the Lord Jesus to be made lower than the angels was truly a downward step.

The Lord's incarnation was an acceptance. When the Lord Jesus became incarnate He came into a new experience and into new conditions. In wonderful love to fallen man the Lord Jesus accepted these conditions. In submission to His Father the Lord was willing to endure misrepresentation, hatred and rejection. The Son from Heaven became the Stranger on earth. Think of the Lord knowing weariness, thirst and pain and accepting too all that His mission on earth would mean for Him. The Lord's incarnation was a voluntary act on His part. It is not merely that He was "made" flesh, but rather He "became" flesh (John 1:14, Newberry margin). He knew before He came what His path on earth would involve and yet, blessed be His Name, He still came. He accepted the lowly circumstances of His birth at Bethlehem. He accepted the manual labour at the carpenter's bench in Nazareth. He accepted the shame experienced at the cross.

The incarnation was a miracle. What could possibly exceed the marvel of the incarnation? In the Lord becoming man He continued to be possessed of Deity. This He never relinquished. Paul writes, "God was manifest in the flesh" (1 Tim 3:16). The very thought of manifestation would immediately suggest a prior existence. The One who was once hidden now comes into manifestation. So much so that John the apostle with an adoring heart could write, "we have heard, ...we have seen with our eyes,...we have looked upon, and our hands have handled, of the Word of life" (1 John 1:1). The miracle consists in the wonderful fact that the Son of God became flesh, was made in the likeness of men and dwelt in a real body of flesh and blood.

The incarnation was a necessity. As early as Genesis 3:15 where we have the first clear promise in the Bible, the incarnation of Christ is anticipated. The Seed of the woman (Christ)) will bruise the head of the serpent (the devil). The incarnation was the first great step in the fulfilment of this. All Old Testament history was a preparation for the incarnation. For God's great programme as to the redemption of man and the overcoming finally of evil, the incarnation had to take place. Without this great wonder of the Godhead there would have been no hope for man and no victory over the devil. The incarnation of Christ was necessary for a number of reasons. We point to three:

1. The REVELATION OF GOD. In the same chapter where John tells us the Lord "became flesh" he also tells us that Christ as the only-begotten Son declares the Father (John 1:18). In the Person of the Incarnate Son, God was made known to men.

2. The REMOVAL OF SIN. On the very first page of the New Testament the great spiritual purpose of the incarnation is stated, "thou shalt call his Name Jesus: for he shall save his people from their sins" (Matt 1: 2 1). The Saviour became man that sinners might be saved.

3. The RULE OF THE EARTH. The incarnation was also necessary because God intended man to have sovereignty over the whole world. Though man lost this dominion due to the fall, God will yet see to it that in the Person of Christ this universal rule will be restored. A man must sit upon the throne in the kingdom. While Psalm 8:4-9 is a song of the past glory that man had, yet Scripture is clear - "he must reign" (1 Cor 15:25) and again God "will judge the world in righteousness by that MAN whom he hath ordained…" (Acts 17:31). So the incarnation was the first most important step towards the fulfilment of prophecy and the ultimate goal to which God is moving, even His dwelling with men in perfect satisfaction, bringing finally to men eternal happiness. The implications of the incarnation are very great indeed and the very fact of it taking place at all causes the soul to rise up in worship and praise.

> Did the Lord a man become
> That He might the law fulfil,
> Bleed and suffer in my room;
> And canst thou, my tongue, be still?

His Sinless Life

Although the subject of Christ's sinlessness has been already briefly touched on in this series, it is of sufficient importance to expand it further. There has been no life like the life of Christ. One has described the lovely life of the Saviour nicely as "a river of silver in a world of soot"! His was a life that stood out conspicuously as morally different. His was the one quite unspotted life lived within a sinful race. There was no inclination in Him to evil, there was no weakness in Him due to the effects of any previous transgressions. He had no shortcomings to acknowledge and had no regrets about any of His words or ways. He never felt Himself personally unfitted for the great mission God had entrusted to Him. In the record of His perfect life we never find Him confessing any sin. Sin brought sickness into the world and death, but, because He was sinless, there never was a day in His life on earth when He had to say, "I am sick" (cp Is 33:24). This unique Man was never "a dying man", for the seeds of corruption and decay were not working in Him. It is truly wonderful to think that for over 12,000 days the Lord Jesus lived in this world without ever sinning. Every single day the holiness of the Saviour was unmarred whether the days were full of duties, home responsibilities, or simply lived in concourse with others. No day was different from another as far as the measure of His holiness was concerned. His perfection did not grow by degrees, but was ever the same in its fulness. It knew no intermission or deficiency.

On such a fundamental subject as this it will be good to consider it by referring to a fourfold testimony all bearing clear witness to His spotless character.

THE WITNESS OF THE PUBLIC

Our blessed Lord did not live in obscurity. His public ministry shows this. Day by day He lived under the full blaze of men's observation and yet they could find no trace or evidence of wrong-doing in Him. It is true that what men thought and concluded about Him is not so valid in comparison with God's estimate, but nevertheless it is of value. While public opinion can change and vary, yet, as the Lord lived His life before men, they could see how different He was. His pure life and character left deep and lasting impressions upon men's conscience and thoughts. Men were meticulous in spying on Him to try to entangle Him in His words and to bring every possible accusation against Him, but all was without success. Not one individual could find anything to fasten on to accuse. The Lord Jesus was really the only person that has ever lived, who, in the fullest sense, was unafraid to live under the close scrutiny of men.

The conscience of Judas, the imagination of Pilate's wife whose sleep was upset, and the judgment of Pilate himself all show the effect the pure character of Christ had on them (Matt 27:4,19,24). "Innocent blood", "that just man" and "this just person" is a threefold cord of individual testimony which is not quickly broken. The dying repentant thief and the centurion soldier could add their testimonies to His blameless character (Lk 23:41,47)

THE WITNESS OF THE APOSTLES

It is one thing to listen to the witness of men even though in some cases it be given unwillingly, but it is quite another matter to listen to the testimony of those who were closest to Christ. The twelve disciples lived daily in His presence for three and a half years. In what way did the Lord impress them? If there had existed, however faintly, in the Lord's mind a consciousness of sin, then it would have affected the Saviour's demeanour, and the disciples would have observed the signs of a bad conscience. If this had been detected it would have certainly modified their estimate of Christ, and this would have been noticeable in the epistles. However, nowhere in the epistles do we find a hint of a doubt as to our Lord's sinlessness, but rather a clear setting forth of the Lord's sinless life. John the apostle was a man that knew our Lord perhaps better than most and experienced the nearest of fellowship with Him. The proverb "familiarity breeds contempt" was far from true in John's attitude to His Master. In looking at the best of men from a distance all may seem good and pleasing, but, when getting to know the person more intimately, faults and blemishes in the character may come to light. John looking back about forty years to the period of time he spent in the company of his Saviour says with a mature conviction, "in Him is no sin" (1 John 3:5). The emphasis here is on the word "sin", so that it reads, "Sin in Him there is none". John also makes it clear that the Lord Jesus was not only pure in His sojourn on earth, but that in His resurrection and exalted state His purity continues. John writes "He IS pure" (1 John 3:3). Peter confirms the witness of His fellow apostle by writing, "Who did no sin, neither was guile found in His mouth" (1 Pet 2:22). Paul, though not a first-hand witness, gives to Christian doctrine a most significant truth:- He "knew no sin" (2 Cor 5:21).

These words should be noted - it means that fully and completely He knew no sin. This verse shows that the sinlessness of Christ has a vital bearing on the substitutionary character of Christ's death. If Christ was not personally free from sin, then He could not take my place as a sinner and my acceptance before God as a believer would be seriously upset.

THE WITNESS OF CHRIST HIMSELF

One day He could challenge His very enemies the Jews to bring home to His own conscience any possible sinful word or act, "which of you convinceth Me of sin?" (John 8:46). The Lord stands and waits for an answer. None it seems comes. The reason why the Lord's teaching was so unique, powerful and authoritative was because He was sinless and, if sinless, His teaching could not be wrong. So He could also ask, "if I say the truth, why do ye not believe me?" Why not indeed! This great statement of Christ reveals that He was personally aware of His own sinlessness. It is right to say that the witness of Christ and of God to the truth of the sinlessness of the Person of Christ is of greater weight. The Lord Jesus could say what no man before Him or after Him could ever say, "the prince of this world cometh and hath nothing in me" (John 14:30).

There was an entire absence of evil inclination in the Lord for the temptations of the devil to lay hold of. It has been said, "this cunning searcher had pried narrowly into every corner of his life; and if there had been anything amiss, would have been sure to have spied it and proclaimed it. But he could find nothing."

Again the Lord could say what the greatest and holiest of God's servants could never say, "I do ALWAYS those things that please him (the Father)" (John 8:29). This shows His clear consciousness of complete and unbroken harmony with the Father. Note the consistency here in the arresting word "always". The Lord's perfect obedience filled the hours of each day with delight for God.

THE WITNESS OF GOD

What was heaven's estimate of this unique Man? It is true that so little is known of the Lord's early days on earth and that believers speak of the "hidden" years of Nazareth. The Christian does not try to pry or speculate as to all that may have happened in those secluded years. He is happy to believe the appraisal of God concerning them, when at Jordan

He stands on the threshold of His public ministry – "This is My beloved Son, in whom I am well pleased" (Mat 3:17). The seal of divine approval is placed upon all those secluded years whether it is the Lord's growing childhood, enquiring boyhood or mature manhood. From God's testimony the believer is confident that, be it in the simple home at Nazareth, at the busy carpenter's bench, or even in His walk among men the revealing search light of God showed every word, action and step to be perfect. Later still on the Mount of Transfiguration the same blessed testimony is given, (Mat 17:5).

The believer can rest assured that in his Lord he has a Saviour that did not sin and could not sin. Upon the incomparable character of Christ rests the value of His atoning sacrifice (Heb 9:14), the blessing before God of our present acceptance (2 Cor 5:21), the reality of His perfect example (1 Pet 2:22) and the power of His sympathy as High Priest (Heb 4:15).

His Death

There has never been a death like the death of Christ. One writer has referred to it as the "death of deaths in the death of Christ". It was certainly no ordinary death. The death of Christ at Calvary stands out as earth's greatest battlefield, as history's greatest moment, as man's foulest deed, and as God's greatest display of love. When the Holy Scriptures are read concerning the death of Christ it becomes very clear that such a death had features which mark it out as so very different from, and far above, any other. When it is compared with the sacrifices of the OT it is described as "better sacrifices" (a plural of excellence being used to set forth its fullness in embracing and fulfilling all the offerings now superseded by His death – Heb 9:23). When compared with ordinary human generosity the Lord's death has a moral elevation in it that is lacking in the best and noblest of human sacrifice for others (see Rom 5:6-8). When compared with the death of mankind, who all must submit to the king of terrors, Christ's death is seen to be entirely of His own volition (cp Eccl 8:8 with Matt 27:50). No less than five times the Lord in John 10 says He gives His life for the sheep. His death was no accident. It was so important to each of the Gospel writers that it caused them to write much about the Lord's suffering. In looking at the Person of Christ in His death it is in every way a most precious, touching and humbling theme to the soul. It will be simply considered in the following three ways.

THE MANNER OF HIS DEATH
His was the worst kind of death. It was a shameful death, being the most painful and degrading form of capital punishment in the ancient world. In the times of the Romans they began to use crucifixion more and more as a deterrent to criminal activity. In the time of our Lord it was a common sight. That the Lord of Glory should choose such an instrument as a cross upon which to suffer is most affecting to say the least. The Lord did not die by stoning or by being cast over the brow of a hill as the Jews attempted to do, but by one of the worst inventions of cruelty ever devised by man. He himself

His Death

knew exactly all the extreme acts of indignity and abuse men would cause Him to suffer. In Luke 18: 32,33 the Lord predicts seven things of His suffering experience, beginning with His being handed over to the Gentiles and ending in His resurrection from the dead. In between we have the various ways that man showed their hatred of Him – the contemptuous insultings, the callous indignities and the cruel injuries. For our blessed Lord the pain and the shame were very real. On the cross on three separate occasions He was offered vinegar mingled with gall (Cp. Matt 27:34, Luke 23:36 and John 19:29,30). The ingredients of this vinegar were an attempt to dull the sense of pain, but the Lord would not have His senses dulled or His mind beclouded. No, He would experience all the horrors of the cross feelingly and fully in His body. Unlike Adam who was caused to go into a deep sleep, our precious, holy Saviour endured all the sufferings of the cross that He might have His bride, the church.

THE MAJESTY OF HIS DEATH

One cannot read the four gospels with any degree of care without coming to see that there was something about the Lord's death so very different and unique from any other. Even in going to the cross the initiative was always in the hands of Christ. It is He that moves towards men and allows them to do what they will. The impression one gets is that He is in control and not men. Consider an example or two which show so wonderfully the majesty of Christ in death. Take the instance when the crowd smote their breasts at such a sight; they had seen strange things that day (Luke 23:48). This was not the effect usually produced upon the people by a public crucifixion. The death of the two thieves on either side of the Lord caused no such emotion. No doubt could possibly exist as to the justice of their punishment, but the Lord's behaviour on the cross was different to that of the thieves and caused deep impressions. Mark emphasises that "He SO cried out and gave up the ghost" (Mark 15:39). This was one of the things which caused the centurion to confess, "Truly this man was the Son of God". That seasoned soldier, who likely attended a number of crucifixions, had never heard anyone cry out like this before. He read in the Lord's voice character and majestic power.

One more detail must suffice. In reading John 19 we see that he is not concerned about the noise around the cross, the darkness, or even the cry of forsaking, but portrays a scene where all seems calm and the Lord is in control. John alone tells us of the title above the cross that was not changed, the coat that was not rent and the legs that were not broken. How does one account for the firmness of Pilate when he had been so fickle before the people earlier? "What I have written I have written". The Lord is clearly in control here. It all shows Him to be the true King, the true Redeemer and the true Passover Lamb. In spite of all that men did to the Lord the majesty of the Son shines through the whole story of the cross in John 19.

THE MYSTERY OF HIS DEATH

There is no mystery in the fact that our Lord really died, but that one who was the Son of God should die on that cross is a mystery that eternity itself will never resolve. It is very true that God cannot die, but that He who died was God. He who suffered there was no other than Jehovah's Fellow (Zech 13:7) - "'Tis mystery all! The Immortal dies", cries Charles Wesley. The supernatural three hours of darkness at the cross show a unique period that was set apart from the gaze of men. All that happened then remains a mystery. The great work of atonement then took place. Just as the work of atonement was done within the seclusion of the holiest of all by Israel's high priest and was witnessed by not another Israelite, so in the darkness the Lord bare our sins. Human eyes, however curious, however callous were not permitted to see the supreme sufferings of the Son of God. Therefore no one can tell us about them. Can we understand how it was that a Divine Person inflicted punishment, or that One endured it? The secret transaction between God and Christ will ever cause the soul to wonder. The Saviour's middle cry on the cross was "My God, my God, why hast thou forsaken me?" We cannot understand this awful cry because we cannot understand fully the awfulness of sin, the holiness of God and greatness of the price the Lord had to pay.

What does His death mean? The Lord's unique death was the perfect sacrifice for sin. No wonder in Hebrews 10:12 it is called "one sacrifice". It stands alone. There has been none like it before or since. It was penal. Scripture says it was for our sins (1Cor 15:3). The Lord's death was not the result of His own misdeeds, for He had none. His death stands in relation to the sins of others. Hebrews again says that He was "once offered to bear the sins of many" (Heb 9:28). The Lord's death was final. It requires no repetition like the sacrifices by Israel of old did. What a blessing and a relief for sin burdened souls to know this today. The Lord's death was efficacious. The Lord being raised from the dead and also exalted to heaven proves in a most wonderful way that this is so. In Hebrews the Lord is seen as sat down (ch 1:3). No priest in Israel was ever provided with a seat. Their work was unceasing. The Lord's death is so efficacious that by it the believer is sanctified or made eternally fit for the presence of God. The Lord's death was glorifying to God. Human beings are so naturally self-centred that it is easy when looking at the death of Christ to see our own standpoint, instead of rather seeing the glory of God in it. No death has ever brought such glory to God as the death of His Son (John 13:31). The death of Christ will forever remain in unfading glory, so that, even in eternity, God will never allow His people to forget the death to which so much is owed. The Saviour is never more precious as when the soul ponders Him suffering on the tree. May God help us to value more and more the One who gave Himself for us.

His Resurrection

The resurrection of Christ is a great foundation truth of the gospel. Without it Christianity is doomed. The faith of the believer is not based on a coffin lid, but upon a Saviour who bodily rose from the dead. The empty garden tomb of Christ tells its own blessed story of the triumph of Christ over sin, Satan and the grave. It is one of the best attested facts in history; yet no one actually witnessed the resurrection itself. The soldiers, the women who went to the grave and the disciples themselves did not see the Saviour rise from the dead. The Gospels do not enter into the modes or details of that mighty event. The apostle Paul says concerning the Lord, "He was buried" (1 Cor 15:4). The fact of Christ's burial coming between His death and resurrection shows two things. It demonstrates that His death was real. It also was a very necessary pre-condition of His physical resurrection. He actually died – so He was buried. He was actually buried – so He actually rose again.

In the Scriptures there are a number of resurrections recorded, but the resurrection of the Lord Jesus was unique. It was different from all others in three particulars. Unlike other persons' resurrections the Lord predicted His own rising from the dead (Matt 16:21 & 17:22-23). No one else who rose from the dead is ever recorded as confidently prophesying their resurrection. Secondly our Lord taught that He would by His own power rise from the dead. It is true that God raised Him from the dead, but it is also incredibly true that the Lord by His own power accomplished it. This is a very great fact that testifies to the deity of our blessed Lord. He could say concerning His life "I have power to lay it down and I have power to take it again" (John 10:18). Let it be clearly stated here that the Lord Jesus was not passive in His resurrection. It is not only that He was raised by the power of another, but that He rose too by His own power. The very thought of it emphasizes the greatness of Christ. Thirdly unlike other resurrections our Lord's was permanent. It was not temporary like that of the resurrection of Lazarus. All those raised from the dead in the Bible would die again, but the Lord Jesus has a "better resurrection" (Heb 11:35). It is better because it is permanent and it is the guarantee that all believers in Him who have died will also be raised to never die again. Those recorded in the Word of God who were raised again were all raised with natural bodies to this mortal life with all its many limitations and indeed miseries. Because of the resurrection of Christ the resurrection of the Christian will be to possess a spiritual body suited for heaven with a glorious freedom from the infirmities of earth (1 Cor 15:44). The resurrection of Christ is the guarantee of the resurrection of the believer (1 Cor 6:14 & 2 Cor 4:14). This is one blessed result of the resurrection of Christ as far as the believer is concerned.

The resurrection of Christ was a great necessity. Our Lord could say Himself, "It behoved Christ to suffer, and to rise from the dead the third day" (Luke 24:46). It is most important to dwell on this and to ask the question why was it so necessary. The following points, showing how essential the Lord's own resurrection was, will be of benefit to the reader.

IT WAS A PERSONAL NECESSITY

The word of the angel to the woman at the grave was "He is not here: for He is risen, as He said" (Matt 28:6). The Lord's own claim that He would rise from the dead was completely vindicated by His resurrection. His own word was at stake. Because of who Christ was it might be justly said that God Himself was morally obliged to raise His Son from the dead. Indeed one of the causes of His resurrection is His own holiness. This is why we read the prophetic words of Christ in the Psalms, "neither wilt Thou suffer Thy Holy One to see corruption" (Psalm 16:10). Peter declares concerning Christ "whom God hath raised up, having loosed the pains of death: because it was not possible that He should be holden by it" (Acts 2:24). It is the holiness of the Lord that constituted the impossibility of His being holden of death,

IT WAS A SCRIPTURAL NECESSITY

A number of OT passages speak prophetically of the resurrection of Christ. Peter on the day of Pentecost claims that David spoke of Christ's resurrection and quotes Psalm 16:8-11, (see Acts 2:25-32). Again Isaiah the prophet clearly speaks of Christ's resurrection when he refers to the Lord being with the rich man in His death and then goes on to speak of the Lord prolonging His days (53:9-11). This can only be understood in the light of the fact of the Lord's resurrection from the dead. Had Christ not risen from the dead then the veracity of the Scriptures would be in great doubt. The marvel is that prophecies uttered centuries before the event were literally fulfilled. The believer can have every confidence that Scripture is true.

IT WAS A GOSPEL NECESSITY

One has only to read the masterly argument of Paul in 1 Cor 15:12-19 to see that without the resurrection of Christ there would be dreadful consequences for the doctrine of the gospel. Its very foundation would be shaken and most untrustworthy. There could be no gospel of hope and forgiveness preached if Christ was still in the grave. Paul shows that if Christ was not raised then apostolic preaching is baseless, faith is futile and the sinner who believes would really be without a Saviour. If the Lord had not been raised then the great sin question would not be settled. How grand to know it is otherwise for Paul exultingly can say, "but now is Christ risen from the dead" (v.20).

A JEWISH NECESSITY

The Word of God predicts a literal future restoration for the nation of Israel. One has only to read Ezekiel 37, Isaiah 60 and Jeremiah 31 to be clear as to this. The Lord Jesus too will be their Messiah and King (Isa 32:1). He will rule in a kingdom of peace and prosperity. If Christ had not been raised then the whole prophetic programme of God would collapse. Israel would have to struggle on as a downtrodden and despised people. There would be no hope of deliverance from their enemies, but God's promise to them stands, "I will give thee the sure mercies of David" (Acts 13:34; Isa 55:3). Paul interprets this as being fulfilled in the resurrection of Christ. So that what God promised to David will yet be fulfilled to him in the future Millennial kingdom. God will establish all for Israel through the Lord Jesus risen and glorified.

A JUDGMENT NECESSITY

The Lord Jesus taught that the Father has committed the judgment of men at the end of time to Him. He also could say that He will be man's future Judge because He is the Son of Man (John 5:22 & 27). The Lord Jesus as a real man will be God's judge throughout His reign in the kingdom (Acts 17:31), and also as a man He will sit on the Great White Throne before Whom the dead small and great shall stand (Rev 20:11-15). If it is not true that Christ's grave is empty then that awful throne will never be set up and the final judgement of the wicked dead will never take place. The throne and the judgment will require the Judge for it to be all solemnly complete. Such an event demands the fact of a Risen Christ. There is nothing more certain that such a dreadful scene will take place not only because the Word of God says so, but also because the resurrection of Christ guarantees it.

The resurrection of Christ is a reality. Being so it should motivate every believer to a greater devotion to the Person of Christ. The chief priests bought the silence of the soldiers guarding the tomb. The last weapon the enemy used was lies. It is not surprising that they paid a great price to get the lame story repeated that the disciples had stolen the body by night (Matt 28:13). It is true that many will give much to suppress Christian Truth, but how much are we giving to support it? We speak not merely in monetary terms, but in spiritual terms of devotion and sacrifice. The enemy has never been successful in obscuring the truth of the resurrection, and it continues on as a triumphant well proven fact.

His Ascension

After His resurrection the Lord Jesus did not ascend to heaven immediately upon rising from the dead. This He easily could have done, but He chose to manifest Himself on different occasions to His own. The fact that He did so shows His great care for the disciples. The forty days between the Lord's resurrection and His ascension to heaven was a necessary period of preparation for the disciples. During this period the Lord showed Himself alive by many infallible proofs (Acts 1:3). The Lord loved His own and was loath to leave the little flock.

The great purpose of the Lord lingering forty days before going to His Father was to prove beyond all doubt the reality of His resurrection. The Lord seemed to suddenly appear at will and just as suddenly disappear. He appeared in a garden, on a road, on a mountain, in a house and on the sea shore. He appeared on the resurrection day itself. He appeared eight days later. He appeared towards the end of the forty days and He appeared on the morning of the fortieth day.

This very significant forty day period was preceded by His resurrection and succeeded by His ascension. At its beginning angels announced His resurrection. At its end angels announced His second advent. The voice they heard (Jn 20:16), the passion marks of His body they saw (Lk 24:39), his eating with them in the upper room (Lk 24:42,43; Acts 10:41) and the miracle on the shore of Galilee (Jn 21), all powerfully testified to His identity. His speech, His scars and His special characteristic actions together tell the wonderful story that the Person the disciples and women saw was no impersonation, but the very same One who had accompanied them in His ministry and endured the suffering of the cross. Mary could say in delightful recognition, "Rabboni". Thomas could say in adoring worship "My Lord and my God". John could say in joyful surprise "It is the Lord". There was no mistaking who He was. No one ever spoke like Him. None but He could show the evidence of His crucifixion. Only the Lord could do what He did in directing the disciples to catch the multitude of fishes.

There are four interesting expressions used in Scripture in describing the ascension. Each of them emphasises a particular aspect of the Lord's Person and are in keeping with either the theme of the writer or the immediate context in which they occur. They are instructive phrases, which sum up beautifully the greatness of the event.

RECEIVED UP

Mark says our Lord was "received up into heaven" (Mk 16:19). Mark is the Gospel of the servant character of Christ. What a fitting end to his Gospel! He shows us here the rewarded Servant. Thus the Ascension of the Lord was His entrance into the reward that the Father had prepared for Him after completing the work given Him to do. Upon His ascension He commenced His session at the right hand of God. Peter says, "Whom the heaven must receive…" (Acts 3:21). The Lord was welcomed in heaven. What a glorious moment it must have been when the Lord ascended right up to the very throne of the heavenly world. It must have filled heaven with rejoicing. The forty day period was a necessary prelude to the Lord's ascension to heaven. The ascension of the Lord was really the completion of His glory. The glorification of the Lord Jesus began at His ascension. His ascension was also the completion of all that was involved in His incarnation. It was a spiritual necessity in order that from heaven His promise to send the Holy Spirit might be fulfilled. He could say, "It is expedient for you that I go away: for if I go not away, the Comforter will not come unto you; but if I depart, I will send him unto you" (Jn 16:7).

CARRIED UP

Luke tells us it was while in the very act of blessing the disciples that He was "parted from them, and carried up into heaven" (Lk 24:51). His hands were lifted up, (v.50). Did they see the wounds in His hands as He did this? The action pictures the priestly ministry of Christ – a ministry still going on! This wonderful event produced a twofold response upon the disciples. It resulted in their worshipping Him and being filled with great joy (v.52). It is Luke's delight to present in his Gospel the perfect, dependent manhood of the Lord. So, consistent with this the Lord's ascension is described as being "carried up". Miraculously the Lord's body was carried up into heaven. He who had in the forty days in the wilderness refused to jump from the highest pinnacle of the temple defying the laws of gravitation, now at the end of another forty days is carried up to the heights of heavenly glory.

TAKEN UP

In Acts 1:9-11 the manner of His going to heaven is told. It was while the disciples beheld that "he was taken up; and a cloud received him out of their sight". Clearly the fact that He was "taken up" shows that the ascension was the act of God. The ascension of Christ to heaven must be considered side by side with the incarnation and the resurrection. It was equally miraculous, setting aside the laws by which nature and man are controlled and demanding the exercise of divine power.

It is wonderful that the Lord Jesus descended from heaven into the world to become an infant of days and that He also should conquer death and rise on the third morning from the grave without having seen corruption. It is no less wonderful that His glorified body should have been taken up into the spiritual and eternal world. The ascension really happened. The ascension was the great sequel to the resurrection. That the Lord should finally take His leave of His disciples in the way He did is most important. Had the Lord just suddenly disappeared as He did so often in His resurrection appearances, His disciples would certainly have wondered what had become of Him and when and where they would next see Him.

The tIme that elapsed between the forty day appearances were for a few hours at most, but this parting from them on the Mount of Olives was final. Unlike the Lord's previous disappearances, for a few moments they actually saw the Lord ascend. It was not an apparition they saw. No, it was a visible, bodily ascension. The ascension did not take place at night. There was no possibility of any doubt as to what had happened. They witnessed it. There was only one ascension of the Lord to heaven. It cannot be that after His resurrection all His subsequent appearances were separate descents from heaven. It was a singular event in the same way that His incarnation and resurrection were. Scripture gives no hint whatsoever of any secret or private ascension of Christ to heaven.

GONE INTO

Peter writing of Christ's ascension says, "Who is gone into heaven, and is on the right hand of God" (1 Pet 3.22). The fact that the Lord has gone up suggests He has done so by His own will and in His own right. This aspect would emphasise His deity. The Lord in John 3.13 could say, "No man hath ascended up to heaven, but he that came down from heaven, even the Son of man which is in heaven".

While it is true that Elijah had ascended up to heaven, yet he had never come down from heaven like the Lord. Neither did he go up to heaven in his own right. God by His almighty power did this. This makes our Lord's ascension unique in that, while it is true it was the act of God, it was also the act of Christ Himself. He could anticipate a number of times in His earthly ministry His ascension, "I go unto the Father" (Jn 14:28; cp 6:62; 7:33 & 16:10). The ascension then of the Lord has made possible two vital and distinct facts which belong to the present dispensation of the Church. One is a Man in the glory and the other is the Holy Spirit in the world. This is the peculiar character of Christianity that should be appreciated by all believers.

> "We did not mark the chosen few
> When Thou didst through the clouds ascend,
> First lift to heaven their wondering view,
> Then to the earth all prostrate bend;
> But we believe that mortal eyes
> Beheld that journey to the skies."

His Enthronement

The Hebrew epistle describes in a wonderful threefold way the exaltation to heaven of the Lord Jesus Christ. The writer carries his readers with him as he follows the Lord's journey and says He "passed into (or through) the heavens" (ch.4.14); He was "made higher than the heavens" (ch.7.26); He has "entered into...heaven itself" (ch.9.24). Given the background of this epistle, which draws much upon the Tabernacle in the wilderness, it may well be that in the three references there is an allusion to the High Priest approaching the sanctuary on the Day of Atonement. The Lord passing through the heavens would answer to the court. Being made higher than the heavens would link with the holy place of the Tabernacle. Entering into heaven itself would be a parallel with the holiest of all where the presence of God was. Unlike the work of the High Priest the Lord did not enter into heaven to obtain pardon. This had already been procured at the cross.

Unlike Aaron He did not carry literal blood into heaven, but He entered heaven in all the value and merit of His own blood. Again, unlike Aaron who needed to go into the holiest yearly, the Lord Jesus entered in once. Aaron's once a year entry was finite and temporary, but the entrance into heaven of the Lord Jesus was infinite, permanent and far more blessed.

A great evidence of the fact that Christ is enthroned in heaven is the descent of the Holy Spirit on the day of Pentecost. This Peter made clear in his preaching; "Therefore being by the right hand of God exalted, and having received of the Father the promise of the Holy Ghost, he hath shed forth this, which ye now see and hear" (Acts 2.33). In the NT there are no less than twenty-six references to Christ being at the right hand of God. The right hand in Scripture is the place of power and of favour. The Lord Jesus is presently seated on the throne of God, not really so much in government, but rather in grace, ministering support and succour to His people down here in all their pressures and needs. This is why the throne is called "the throne of grace" (Heb 4.16). It must not be thought that the Lord Jesus is inactive at the right hand of God. He fills, in the presence of God, a number of vital functions for His people. The importance of the present position of Christ at the right hand of God cannot be overstated. His being at the right hand of God in exaltation is the assurance of some great truths of Christianity. A few of these will now be considered briefly.

MATTHEW 22.44 - HIS ENTHRONEMENT IS THE PROOF OF HIS DEITY

In vv. 41 to 46 Christ left the Jews on the horns of a dilemma. Citing from Psalm 110.1, He asks how the Messiah could be David's Lord (i.e. God) when He is his Son. This Scripture is referred to in the NT with varying emphasis, but the Lord here draws special attention to the title "Lord". Here the word is in the singular and without doubt points to the pre-incarnate Lord - a distinct and unique Person in the Godhead. This Psalm is applied to Christ a number of times in the NT. Christ descended from David and yet was before David! No wonder the teachers of the day had no answer to this mystery. The writer in Hebrews 1.13 uses the second part of Psalm 110.1 to prove the deity of Christ; "But to which of the angels said he at any time, Sit on my right hand". This is the climax of the writer's argument in the chapter. He has quoted OT Scripture to prove the deity of Christ and now from Psalm 110 he shows that Christ is God from the fact that He has been invited to enthrone Himself in heaven. Could a mere creature occupy such an exalted position? What a wonderful revelation Psalm 110 is. It is as if David the author was transported to the very throne-room in heaven to hear Jehovah speak to His Son.

HEBREWS 1.3 - HIS ENTHRONEMENT IS THE EVIDENCE THAT HIS SACRIFICE IS EFFICACIOUS

"When He had made purification of sins, [He] sat down on the right hand of the Majesty on high" (RV). Being God, a heavenly throne is a place that fits the Son, and having made purification for sin He deserves it. That the Lord has sat down is the seventh profound statement that the writer makes concerning the Son in these opening verses of Hebrews. How appropriate! One proof that the sacrifice on the cross was final and sufficient is the fact of the enthronement of Christ. How blessed for the believer to know that the Lord Jesus has met every demand of God's throne concerning sin. Every question raised by sin has been fully answered. His sacrifice is sufficient to cleanse every sin of the sinner and take him into the presence of God. What a message this was for the Hebrews! The temporary and repeated offerings of Judaism have been superseded by the once for all sacrifice of Christ. The One who made this offering has been given the highest place in the sunshine and honour of God's presence in Heaven.

ROMANS 8.34 - HIS ENTHRONEMENT IS THE GUARANTEE OF THE SECURITY OF THE BELIEVER

In this precious verse Paul is showing that the security of the believer is permanent. This glorious challenge presents Christ in the full extent of His work from the cross to His present activity. Paul says, "Who is he that condemneth? It is Christ that died, yea rather, that is risen again, who is even at the right hand of God, who also maketh intercession for us". Paul argues in a masterly way from the aspect of the believer's relationship to Christ. The Lord's past and present acts are not only the warrant of His love, but also the assurance of the believer's security in Christ. The fact that He is now at the right hand of God tells its own story that Christ has triumphed over sin and Satan. So long as He is up there beside His Father and continues in His intercession, the believer need fear no possibility of condemnation. The believer only needs to look up by faith to His Saviour at the right hand of God and all is settled.

MARK 16.20 - HIS ENTHRONEMENT GIVES ASSURANCE OF POWER IN SERVICE

Mark shows here that the Lord's great earthly work is over. His faithful service had been finished to the satisfaction of God. Now we have the reward for this unique Servant – "He was received up into heaven, and sat down on the right hand of God" (v.19). Men had refused His work on earth, but now He takes His seat in a place that indicates power. Is the Lord inactive on this throne? No, replies Mark, the Lord is still working and doing so through His servants on earth. Therefore the toiling labourer for God can go forth knowing he has the help of his Lord. Oh that each servant of the Lord would know more of this power coming down from the enthroned Lord. The very experience of this power is an evidence of Christ being at the right hand of God.

HEBREWS 12.2 - HIS ENTHRONEMENT IS THE ENCOURAGEMENT FOR THE BELIEVER'S PILGRIM JOURNEY

The throne of grace upon which our blessed Lord is seated is the throne of His essential Deity. It is the throne of His everlasting Priesthood. It is the throne of His exalted Manhood, but not only is it all these, it is also the throne of His encouraging Example and Leadership. Hence the Hebrew writer exhorts his readers to be "looking [off] unto Jesus, the author and finisher of...faith; who for the joy that was set before him endured the cross, despising the shame, and is set down at the right hand of the throne of God". They are to look off or away from the great worthies of ch.11 to

Jesus enthroned. In ch.11 faith was never carried through to perfection. Faith among these great men was scattered in fragments, each saint showing some particular aspect, but Jesus had all faith. He traversed the whole extent and realm of faith. Through all His earthly pathway and right to the end He trusted in God and never failed. If believers are tempted to despondency or feel like giving up then we are encouraged to look unto Jesus. Occupation with this enthroned One who knew so much opposition, suffering and trial is the grand antidote to discouragement.

His Present Ministry

The session of the Lord Jesus at the right hand of God in heaven, which began at His ascension, continues to the present hour. The present age of grace is characterised by His patience. The "patience of Christ" (RV) referred to by Paul in 2 Thessalonians 3.5 is not the patience which He showed on earth, but His present attitude of waiting in heaven. It is true that the interval between the ascension and the Lord coming for His Church at the Rapture lengthens century by century, but believers take heart from the fact that the seated Christ in heaven is waiting for the moment when He will come to claim His Bride. As Christ waits seated on the throne, so believers wait with Him. Is the reader truly waiting for Him? As seated in heaven, all pain and sorrow for Him are over. Yet the sitting of Christ is much more than this for it tells of His victory. This is seen in His own words to the Church at Laodicea in Revelation 3. 21 (RV), "I will give to him to sit down with me in my throne, as I also overcame, and sat down with my Father in his throne". Our Lord in His present session never rests from the ongoing activities upon which the Church is so dependent. It is said of Pethahiah of Nehemiah's day that he was "at the king's hand in all matters concerning the people" (Neh 11.24). Just as he fulfilled a vital role while the people engaged in the work, so our Lord Jesus in His present ministry in heaven is performing functions that are indispensable. Three present ministries of Christ will be briefly touched upon.

HIS PRIESTHOOD

In the Epistle to the Hebrews no aspect of the Lord's heavenly ministry is more insisted upon than His priestly office and work. It might be asked why the believer needs the Lord as High Priest. The answer to this is at least twofold. The High Priesthood of Christ is needed to render the service of the believer acceptable to God. This is seen in type in Exodus 28.38 where it is mentioned that Aaron was to "bear the iniquity of the holy things". The best of Israel's service and the best of their offerings would never have been accepted apart from this wonderful provision. The believer's service today is imperfect. His prayers are defective and his worship often even in the holiest moments comes from a heart adversely affected by sin, but through the priestly mediation of Christ in heaven all is presented to God in perfection. Then again the Lord's Priesthood sustains the worship of His people within the holiest and through His priestly ministry the believer is able to draw near to God. The key statement of Hebrews is found in ch.7.19 - "we draw nigh unto God". This stands at the centre of the epistle. The introduction of the better hope in place of the law means that what the former priesthood could not do the Lord by His powerful and more efficient Priesthood has accomplished. The congregation of Israel had to remain outside while their high priest went within the earthly sanctuary. Now, however, all believers may enter the holiest in heaven. Through the Lord's ministry as Priest every believer can enjoy direct access to God. Believers should experience for themselves this blessing and often be found in God's presence.

Among the many contrasts in Hebrews 7 between the Jewish priesthood and the Lord's is that the Aaronic order was a succession of dying men who served in a temporary system, whereas the believer's great High Priest is alive for evermore (v.24). Because death interrupted, their *number* was many, but our Lord is one singular Priest who will never die. Second, the believer's High Priest is not like the Levitical high priests, a sinner, but rather "holy, harmless, undefiled" (v.26). Here we have the present characteristics of Christ showing His superior qualifications to be the High Priest of His people. Because of their sin the priests of old had *need*. Hence they had to offer for their own sins (v.27). Our blessed Lord had no such need. Third, the Levitical priests were only men, but the Great High Priest of Christianity stands in a unique relationship to God. He is "the Son" (v.28). So the writer in the last verse of Hebrews 7 emphasises the *nature* of the priests of Judaism. The Lord is not only man, but also the very Son of God. As the believer journeys through the wilderness of this world it is comforting to know that there is a sympathetic High Priest in Heaven.

HIS ADVOCACY

While the Lord's Advocacy is closely linked with His Priesthood, it is, at the same time, distinct from it. The apostle John writes, "And if any man sin, we have an advocate with the Father, Jesus Christ the righteous" (1 Jn 2.1). His Priesthood has to do with God. His Advocacy has to do with the Father. His Priesthood has more to do with our infirmities. His Advocacy has more to do with our sins. His Priesthood has to do with approach to God. His Advocacy has to do with fellowship with the Father. The word "advocate" simply means, "one drawn along side to help". This is exactly what the Lord is doing for us in heaven. It does not say that the Lord's Advocacy is for those who confess their sins. The ministry of the Lord as Advocate begins as soon as a believer sins. It means that He meets all charges that lie against the believer on the score of sin. Sin may disturb the believer's communion with the Father, yet still the Lord Jesus Christ maintains the union of every believer with the Father. While there is a clear type of the Lord's Priesthood, it would be hard to find a type of His Advocacy in the OT. The reason for this is that advocacy is a new thought additional to priesthood. In reality it is a new ministry. It is a wonderful truth revealed to the family and distinct to the family of God. John is the family epistle and it is in this epistle and nowhere else in the NT that this ministry of Christ is presented. It points to the completeness of Christ's work on behalf of His people.

Every believer needs Christ as an Advocate. This fact should be plain enough from 1 John 2.1. The existence of such a ministry destroys the idea, still propounded by some, of the believer's sinless perfection. Upon what does His success as our Advocate depend? Three great truths give to Christ's Advocacy a force, which assures the believer of acceptance. His ministry as Advocate rests on His *communion* with the Father. The Lord, now in the presence of His Father, is enjoying face to face communion with Him. He is always there for us. His ministry as Advocate rests on His *character* for He is "Jesus Christ the righteous". His ministry as Advocate rests also on His *cross work* - "He is the propitiation for our sins" (v.2). All these aspects combine for His effective work as the Advocate.

HIS INTERCESSION

If as Priest Christ represents the believer before God, and as Advocate He undertakes the believer's cause, then as Intercessor He furthers the believer's petitions. God has given His people a full provision in the present heavenly ministry of Christ. There are two passages in the NT directly referring to Christ's ministry of intercession. In Romans 8.34 His intercession is seen as a climax to all His saving activities. His death, resurrection and exaltation all culminate in this ministry. It is not only that our trust is in a Christ that died, nor on a Christ that lives, nor even on an exalted Christ in heaven, but on the wonderful knowledge that this glorious Person uses His opportunity in being at God's right hand to plead our case before God. The other passage that speaks of the Lord as the Intercessor is Hebrews 7.25. The intercession of Christ is vitally linked with, and depends upon, the Lord's Priesthood. Since the Lord is a Priest forever, His intercession for believers is permanent. He will never give place to another - "He ever liveth to make intercession for them".

The very purpose of the Lord's life in heaven is that He may intercede on the believer's behalf. It is not simply that the Lord continues to offer one long prayer throughout the whole duration of His High Priestly life. The picture of the Lord approaching with outstretched hands a reluctant God is surely not the thought here. Rather His very being in the presence of God and His very life in heaven is His prayer. Let every believer be encouraged by the knowledge that they have a heavenly Intercessor.

His Second Coming

The Word of God can be justly called a "prophetic book". It has been estimated that a quarter of the Holy Scriptures is prophetic, or, to put it another way, of the 31,724 verses in the Bible 8,352 of these are predictive. The only reliable source then of information as to future times is the inspired Word of God. There is no doubt that Christ came the first time into the world. This is a fact of history. If He came, lived, died, rose again and went back to heaven, will He come back again? The answer to this question is a decided YES. When the Lord Jesus ascended up to heaven from the Mount of Olives the message of the angels was "this same Jesus, which is taken up from you into heaven, shall so come in like manner" (Acts 1.11). God says He will again bring His Firstbegotten into the world (Heb 1.6). Just as surely as our Lord came the first time He will also come the "second time" (Heb 9.28).

THE TWO STAGES OF HIS SECOND COMING

From a careful reading of the NT it should be seen that the Second Coming will be in two stages. First the Lord Himself will come into the air to catch away the Church (1 Thess 4. 13 to 17). In the second stage He will come to the Mount of Olives to scatter the enemies of Israel and set up His kingdom (Zech 14.4 & Rev 19.11 to 21). Before the Lord comes to the earth the Church is seen in heaven in Revelation 19.7 & 8. How did the Church get there? It can only be that sometime previously she has been caught up to heaven to be in the presence of Christ. There are not two Second Comings, but one which will be in two stages. The first stage is the Rapture of the Church. The second stage is the Revelation of the Lord to the earth. To illustrate this it can be said that the first coming of the Lord into the world was in two stages. The first was when He was born at Bethlehem. Few knew about this. The second stage was later when He entered publicly as the King into Jerusalem. On this occasion many saw Him. So this will be true of the two stages of the Second Coming. In Enoch also there is an illustration of these two stages. Enoch was translated to heaven before the flood. This is a lovely picture of the Church being caught up to heaven before the judgments of the tribulation period set in. But Enoch

His Second Coming

also prophesied that the Lord will come to judge the ungodly in His second advent to the earth (Jude v.14). So Enoch's *translation* pictures the first stage of the Lord's Second Coming - the Rapture, and his *testimony* shows the truth of the second stage of the Second Coming – the Revelation to the earth. The Rapture has in view the blessing of the Church. The Revelation has in view the blessing of the nation of Israel and their deliverance from the Anti-Christ. To make this clear look at 2 Thessalonians 2.1 and 8. In v.1 Paul speaks about the gathering together unto Him. This will take place at the Rapture, but in v.8 he speaks about the man of sin being destroyed by the brightness of His Coming (or Presence). Note the difference. The purpose of the first phase of His Coming in v.1 is for the blessing of His Church, but in v.8 the purpose of the second phase of His Coming is for defeat of the enemy. Let us now briefly touch upon the first stage of the Lord's Second Coming with particular focus on the Person of Christ.

THE RAPTURE WILL BE SUPERNATURAL IN ITS OCCURRENCE

The Lord's descent to the air for His Church will take place in a moment. It will happen suddenly. This is implied in the word "caught up" in 1 Thessalonians 4.17. It means to snatch up or away by an act of divine power. The event of the Rapture will pave the way for a series of solemn happenings on earth, which are outlined in Revelation chs. 6 to 18. There is nothing in 1 Thessalonians 4 to suggest that it will be public or visible. Only believers will respond to the shout of the Lord and be transported to meet Him in the air. Notice the Saviour is called "Jesus" in v.14, speaking of the historical facts of His death and resurrection. Those who believe in the miracle of the resurrection will take part in the miracle of the Rapture. He is called "Lord" in v.16. It is truly wonderful that the Lord Himself will come for His Church and not any angel. His authority is seen in His Lordship. As Lord He is able to descend to the very domain of the Devil – the air. The great adversary will not be able to prevent the Rapture taking place. For one glorious moment in the air Christ will show a completed Church.

THE RAPTURE WILL BE IMPARTIAL IN ITS CHARACTER

Notice again that the Saviour is referred to as "Christ" in v.16. Paul speaks of the "dead in Christ" being raised at the Rapture. This is important because had Paul said the "dead in the Lord", the idea taught by some that only a certain superior and spiritual class of believers will be caught up at the Rapture might have had some credence. The term "in Christ" is a great Pauline expression and speaks of the union of every believer in Christ. It is a positional truth that is true of every believer and not a select few. At the Rapture it will not be a question of *what* we are, but *whose* we are. All who are Christ's therefore will go at the Rapture (1 Cor 15.23). The Rapture will only be selective in that all who are saved will go and all who are not will be left behind. It is vital to understand that participation in the Rapture does not rest upon our attainment, but rather upon His atonement (see 1 Thess 5.7 & 8).

THE RAPTURE WILL BE PRE-TRIBULATIONAL IN ITS TIMING

The Lord's coming for the Church will be pre-tribulational and pre-millennial. The Lord's care for His Church, the Bride, will be such that He will not allow her to pass through the awful period of the day of wrath upon earth. He will come for His Church as the Deliverer from the coming dispensation of wrath (1 Thess 1.10). In 1 Thessalonians 4 Paul tells us WHO we will be meeting in the air - the Lord Himself. In ch.5 he tells us WHAT we will be missing on the earth – the awful day of the Lord and inevitable destruction (vv.2 & 3). Joseph was linked with Asenath his bride before the seven-year period of famine and before he put his brethren through tests to bring them to acknowledge their guilt. It is interesting to see that Asenath is no longer actively mentioned after Genesis ch. 41. She seems to disappear. It is like Revelation chs. 6 to 18 where there is no mention of the Church because it has been caught up to heaven. Where was Asenath? She was obviously being cared for in the palace by Joseph and knew nothing of the famine. So our blessed Lord will take care of His Bride in heaven during the whole course of the seven-year period of the tribulation.

THE RAPTURE WILL BE JOYFUL IN ITS EXPERIENCE

Paul states that at the Rapture the dead who are raised and the living who remain will be caught up to "meet the Lord in the air". What a wonderful moment this will be! It is not that the Lord, having caught up His Church to the air, will then continue His journey downwards to the earth. No! From the air the Church will be taken to the Father's house (Jn 14.2). This word "meet" is the same used of the brethren meeting Paul at Appii Forum (Acts 28.15). What happened on that occasion? Well, the brethren escorted him back to Rome from where they had set out. The use and not the meaning of the word illustrate exactly what will happen when the Lord comes for the Church. We will meet Him in the air and then he will accompany us back to heaven from whence He descended. The blessed sequel of the Rapture is, "so shall we ever be with the Lord". What exceeding joy there will be not only in the re-uniting of believers, who have gone on before, but to see the Lord, be with the Lord and like the Lord forever. What blessed contemplation, companionship and conformity will be the portion of every believer then.

His Second Advent and Millennial Reign

The second stage of the Second Coming of our Lord Jesus Christ will be His advent to the earth. The Lord Jesus, according to the prophetic Word, will certainly come to this earth and set up the throne of His rule and authority. What will happen when He comes to the earth? First we see the **sword** in His hand to smite the foe (Ps 45.3 & Rev 19.11-16). Next the **sickle** is seen in His hand to reap the harvest of the earth (Rev 14.14-16). By comparing this with Joel 3.12-14 it will be understood that the scene applies to the judgment of the living nations. Then the Lord will sit upon the throne of His glory, separating between those that have accepted or rejected the gospel of the kingdom (Mt 25.31-46). This will occur after Christ has descended to the earth and just prior to the inauguration of the kingdom. Finally the **sceptre** is found in His hand (Ps 45.6), a symbol of rule, when He will commence to reign in His millennial kingdom.

In the main there are three great reasons why Christ will come a second time to the earth. Let us consider these.

HE WILL COME TO CONQUER THE ENEMY

In His David character our Lord will come to the earth as a man of war (Is 42.13). He will deal a fatal blow to His and Israel's enemies. Something of this is seen in the solemn prophetic vision of the apostle John in Revelation 19.11-21. The campaign of Armageddon will reach an awful crisis in a final battle in and around Jerusalem. The ungodly confederacy headed by the Anti-Christ and representative of the pride and power of the world will come against little Israel seeking to exterminate them forever. They will say, "Come, and let us cut them off from being a nation; that the name of Israel may be no more in remembrance" (Ps 83.4). Then, just when all hope for the nation seems gone, the Lord, as the Deliverer out of Zion, will appear to their rescue. What a *fright* the world will have when He comes and "treadeth the winepress of the fierceness and wrath of Almighty God" (v.15). What a *feast* the birds of prey will have (v.18). How immense the number of the slain will be. The Lord will completely destroy the enemy. What a *force* Satan will have when the Lord comes to conquer (v.19). He will mobilise his armies against Christ, but it will be utter foolishness to make war with Him! There can be no sustained conflict against this mighty Warrior-King. What a *fate* the beast and the false prophet will have when He appears (v.20). They will not be killed as the others. They are taken and cast alive into the lake of fire to be its first inhabitants. How exceedingly solemn this is! In this vision of John the seer there is no lengthy description of the battle, attention is rather drawn to this great Victor. There are four designations of the Lord Jesus in this Second Advent vision. They contrast very sharply with the four names of the archenemy of souls (ch. 20.2)! In the consistency of His character He is the Faithful and True (v.11). In the mystery of His being He has a name written that no man knew, but He Himself (v.12). In the deity of His Person He is the Word of God (v.13), not now revealing God in grace as He did in His first coming, but revealing God in judgment as He deals with the enemy. In the universality of His rule He is KING OF KINGS AND LORD OF LORDS (v.16).

HE WILL COME TO CONVERT THE NATION OF ISRAEL

In His Joseph character the Lord will come to the earth to convert Israel. In the wonderful story of Joseph we see him winning his brethren, producing their repentance and restoring them unto himself. The Lord Jesus likewise will deal with the nation of Israel. The prophet Zechariah speaks of such a time in Israel's history, "They shall look upon me whom they have pierced, and they shall mourn for him, as one mourneth for his only son" (Zech 12.10). The rest of the passage speaks of the widespread, intense and individual contrition of soul that the Spirit of grace will accomplish in the nation.

The Lord, in coming to earth in all His glory, will bring in times of refreshing from the presence of the Lord (Acts 3.19). This, after the terrible heat of the tribulation, will be a blessing to the whole world and especially to Israel. These times of refreshing refer to the actual arrival of the Lord to Israel to bring relief and a breathing space, as it were, at the end of the great tribulation period. His coming to them will be like a breath of fresh air and as the cool breeze of the morning invigorating them after a long night of suffering in the tribulation. The air of earth will have been filled with the heated atmosphere of God's judgments, but Oh what blessings will be brought to them when the Lord comes! While the figure of the cool breeze

His Second Advent and Millennial Reign

points to one aspect of blessing the Lord's arrival to Israel will bring, Malachi uses another expressive figure to speak of the blessing the Messiah will be to the nation. He says, "The Sun of righteousness (will) arise with healing in his wings" (Mal 4.2). The emphasis now shifts from coolness to warmth and light. This title of the Lord belongs to the Second Advent of Christ as the context in Malachi plainly supports. It suggests the dawn of a new age when He comes. As the Sun of righteousness the Lord Jesus will impart light, joy and healing to the nation. He will effect a spiritual healing in the nation. They will take up the language of Isaiah 53.5, "With His stripes we are *healed*". The nation will be cured and converted. The faithful remnant in Israel, looking forward during the tribulation time to the coming of Israel's true King, will also be able to sing, "The dawn draws nigh, the midnight shadows flee, O what a sunrise will that advent be". Israel will have a new soil, for the land will be fruitful (Ezek 36.35-36) and a new sanctuary in the millennial temple (Ezek chs. 40-48), but, best of all, in Christ they will have a new Sovereign.

HE WILL COME TO CONTROL THE WORLD

He will come in His Solomon character to rule in wisdom and righteousness. Solomon's reign was one of peace. It typifies the millennial reign of Christ. For Satan the whole course of the one thousand year reign of Christ will be a time of restraint in the abyss (Rev 20.1-3). This is one great reason why there will be universal peace in the world. In addition, the great secret of such widespread undisturbed peace will be that one will only shall be bowed to. This will be the will of Jehovah expressed through Christ the King. So we read, "The Lord shall be king over all the earth: in that day shall there be one Lord, and his name one" (Zech 14.9). For the world it will be a period of righteousness. This will be the character of the reign of Christ – "a king shall reign in righteousness" (Is 32.1). For the nations it will be a unique time of rest. War will cease (Ps 46.9). For Israel it will be a time of restoration and rejoicing under the benign reign of the Messiah. This reign will lead into the everlasting kingdom of our Lord and Saviour Jesus Christ (2 Pet 1.11).

What amazing contrasts there will be between the Lord's first coming into the world and His Second Coming. No longer will He be seen as a babe wrapped in swaddling clothes, but He will come with garments dipped in blood. No longer His feet nailed as on the cross, but He will tread His enemies beneath His feet. No longer will men take up stones to stone Him, but they will cry to the stones and rocks to fall on them to hide them from His wrath. No longer will He be smitten with a reed, but He will rule with a rod of iron. No longer will wicked soldiers bow the knee in mockery, but mighty armies will cringe before Him. No longer will He wear the crown of thorns, for on His head will be many diadems. No longer will He come to the Mount of Olives alone (Jn 7.53 & 8.1), but He will come to the same mountain with myriads of His saints (Zech 14.4).

> Lo, He comes! With clouds descending,
> Once for favoured sinners slain;
> Thousand thousand saints attending
> Swell the triumph of His train;
> Hallelujah!
> Jesus comes, and comes to reign!